12-99 RO170788 5
22

DISCARD

Tundra

Philip Steele

 Carolrhoda Books, Inc. / Minneapolis

All words that appear in **bold** are explained in the glossary that starts on page 30.

Photographs courtesy of: The Hutchison Library 20; / Christina Dodwell 5b; / Sergei Buzasovski 22t; Impact Photos / Ken Graham 7t, 9t, 26b; / Alain le Garsmeur 9bl, 11b, 21t; / Geray Sweeney 14t; / Neil Morrison 26t; / Robert Harding Picture Library 22b; / Tony Waltham - cover, 5t, 9br; / Brian Hawkes 17b; / Fred Klus 19; Still Pictures / Tony Rath - title page; / Roland Seitre 4, 11t, 12b, 18b; / Klein/Hubert 7b, 13b, 16b, 17t, 18t; / Thierry Thomas 8; / Peter Prokosch 12t; / Olivier Langrand 13t; / Brigitte Marcon 14b; / J.J. Alcalay 16t; / B & C Alexander 21b, 23; / Andre Maslennikov 24; / Robert Valarcher 25b; / Al Grillo 25t, 27.

Illustrations and maps by David Hogg.

This edition first published in the United States in 1996 by Carolrhoda Books, Inc.

A ZOË BOOK

Copyright © 1996 Zoë Books Limited. Originally produced in 1996 by Zoë Books Limited, Winchester, England.

Carolrhoda Books, Inc., c/o The Lerner Group
241 First Avenue North, Minneapolis, MN 55401

Library of Congress Cataloging-in-Publication Data

Steele, Philip.
  Tundra / Philip Steele.
    p. cm. — (Geography detective)
  "A Zoë book" — T.p. verso.
  Includes index.
  Summary: Describes the tundra regions of the world and how plants, animals, and people live there.
    ISBN 1-57505-040-4 (lib. bdg. : alk. paper)
    1. Tundras — Juvenile literature. 2. Tundra ecology — Juvenile literature. [1. Tundras. 2. Tundra ecology. 3. Ecology.] I. Title. II. Series.
  GB572.S74 1997
  574.5'2644 — dc20   96-10914

Printed in Italy by Grafedit SpA.
Bound in the United States of America
1 2 3 4 5 6 01 00 99 98 97 96

Contents

What Is Tundra?

Imagine a vast, flat landscape. In the short summers, the snow melts into pools of sparkling water. Beautiful wildflowers and other low-growing plants spring up among the grasses. In the long, dark winters, freezing winds whistle over the icy ground. No trees can grow here.

● The word *tundra* comes from the Finnish word *tunguri* and the Sami (Lappish) word *tundar,* which refer to rolling, treeless plains.
● The Arctic tundra stretches over about 5 million square miles and covers almost 9 percent of the earth's total land area.

◀ Tundra lands stretch across northern Russia. Rocks and soils, plants, wildlife, and humans are all affected by the harsh conditions of the tundra.

This region is the Arctic tundra. It lies between the **taiga**—a belt of northern, evergreen forests— and the frozen waters of the Arctic Ocean.

Smaller areas of tundra exist in other parts of the world, too. Tundra can be found in Antarctica and near the tops of very high mountains. Mountain tundra is called alpine tundra. It lies above the alpine **tree line**, where conditions are too harsh for trees to grow. Only plants that can live on bare rock or in thin soils grow here.

◀ Snow covers high mountain peaks all year. Tundra conditions are found between the **snow line** and the alpine tree line below.

◀ A few shrubs and trees do grow in the southern part of the Arctic tundra. Icy winds lash the tundra trees, which grow small and stunted.

Geography Detective

What is the landscape like where *you* live? How is it different from the tundra? What kinds of plants do you think would grow best in your neighborhood? Would they be evergreen trees, trees that lose their leaves in winter, palm trees, or cactuses? Which of these would you find in the tundra? Why or why not?

Where in the World?

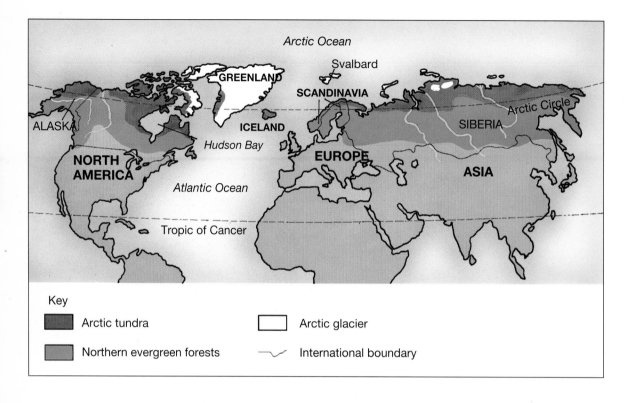

If you look in an atlas, you will see lines running east to west and north to south across the maps. These lines, called **latitude** and **longitude**, are measured in degrees. Most of the world's tundra lies north of the **equator** between the latitudes of 80° and 60° North. Some tundra is found south of the equator between 70° and 55° South.

In North America, the Arctic tundra stretches from northern Alaska to Greenland far to the east. In Europe the Arctic tundra zone covers northern Scandinavia and the bleak moors (plains) of Iceland. Tundra borders the Arctic shores of Russia, stretching eastward across the Russian territory of Siberia. This territory covers the northern half of the Asian continent and has wide, treeless plains crossed by broad rivers.

Tundra is also found in southern latitudes, near Antarctica. However, most of this part of the world

▲ The Arctic tundra zone stretches around the globe. It includes land in the far north of the continents of North America, Europe, and Asia.

▶ Mount McKinley (20,320 ft) is the highest peak in North America. Its snowy slopes tower above the tundra in Denali National Park in Alaska.

▼ In summer in Greenland, snow melts from the tundra. Lakes, pools, and rivers are full to the brim.

is made up of ocean rather than land. The only tundra areas there are on part of the Antarctic Peninsula and on some remote islands, such as South Georgia.

Geography Detective

Look up the world's northern tundra zone (80°–60° North) in an atlas. Using the atlas and the map on page 6, find and name eight countries with tundra lands.

Seasons and Climate

Summer lasts only three or four months in the northern tundra. Even then the temperature rarely rises above 50° F. Some places remain below freezing all summer, and patches of snow cling to the ground. The long, dark winter soon returns. By January temperatures may average anywhere from −4° F to a bitter −22° F.

Conditions vary from one tundra region to another. In northern Scandinavia, winter temperatures may average 18° F, while in eastern Siberia they plunge below −40° F. The winds can be fierce and there is little natural shelter.

The climate varies for a number of reasons. If the tundra lies high above sea level or is a long way from a seacoast, the weather may be extremely cold. Near the sea, **ocean currents** affect the tundra. For example, the North Atlantic Drift warms the coast of northern Scandinavia, while the Labrador Current chills the coast of northeastern Canada.

● Rivers in Siberia freeze so hard in winter that truck drivers can use the waterways as roads.

● Summers can be surprisingly warm on the Canadian tundra. Sometimes people can even swim in Arctic waters. In 1989 the temperature soared to 93° F at Coppermine in the territory of Nunavut!

◀ As our planet travels around the sun, the earth's angle changes. When Arctic lands tilt away from the sun, the northern tundra enters its long winter. At midwinter the sun rises for only a short period every day. At the same time, the southern tundra swings toward the sun. During the short summer, the sun shines almost continually. This picture shows the sun rising on a winter day in Antarctica.

▶ Bright streaks of colored light sometimes flicker in the sky over northern tundra regions. These northern lights (right) are also known as the aurora borealis. The aurora australis, or southern lights, shine over southern tundra regions.

▼ This chart shows the average temperature and precipitation at Old Crow, Yukon, in Canada.

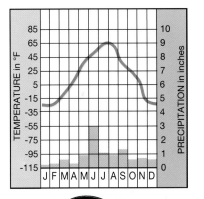

Case Study

The Yukon River rises in northwestern Canada and flows 1,979 miles through the Yukon Territory and Alaska to the Bering Sea. The river flows through forested mountain valleys, **wetlands**, and tundra.

In January the average temperature in the Yukon tundra may drop to −22° F. The wind is full of ice crystals. Between June and August, the temperature becomes warmer, rising above 50° F. Very little **precipitation** falls during the year. In midsummer **drought** may occur.

Geography Detective

Look at these two pictures of the Yukon tundra (right) and the climate chart (above). What might the temperature have been when the winter picture was taken? What might it have been when the summer picture was taken? Is the tundra drier in winter or in summer? How has summer changed the landscape? What has happened to the plant life?

In winter the Yukon tundra is a harsh world of frost and icy winds.

The Yukon tundra in summer is warm, but the risk of frost is never far away.

A Frozen Landscape

Underground the tundra stays frozen all year round. The layer of permanently frozen soil is called **permafrost**. This layer may be frozen as deep as 900 feet or more below the surface.

In Siberia the permafrost is more than 3,000 feet deep in some places. The depth of the permafrost depends on the local climate and on the amount of plant cover that blankets the surface.

The warmth of the summer sun thaws only the top few inches of frozen soil each year. This is called the **active layer**. The frozen soil below is called the **inactive layer**. As the ice melts, the soil of the active layer becomes wet and waterlogged.

When water freezes, the ice takes up more space than the water did. So when water in soil freezes, the soil expands. When the ice melts, the soil contracts, or shrinks. In the tundra, water in the active layer of the soil freezes and thaws with the seasons. The expanding and contracting cause rocks and soils to crack and crumble. The ground may rise up or slip down, pushing boulders and pebbles apart or piling them into heaps.

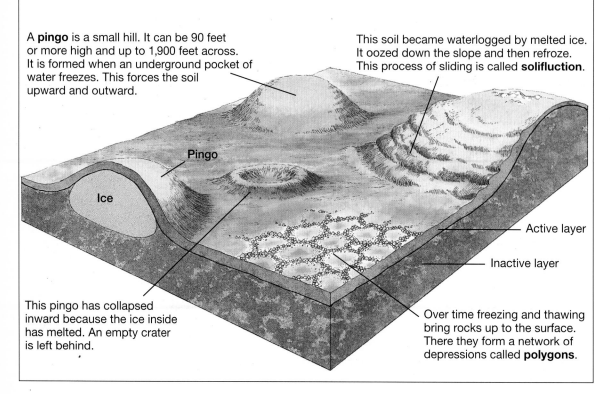

A **pingo** is a small hill. It can be 90 feet or more high and up to 1,900 feet across. It is formed when an underground pocket of water freezes. This forces the soil upward and outward.

This soil became waterlogged by melted ice. It oozed down the slope and then refroze. This process of sliding is called **solifluction**.

Pingo

Ice

This pingo has collapsed inward because the ice inside has melted. An empty crater is left behind.

Active layer

Inactive layer

Over time freezing and thawing bring rocks up to the surface. There they form a network of depressions called **polygons**.

▶ Tundra soil expands and contracts with the seasons. The movement creates **patterned ground**, or a maze of cracks and shapes in the soil.

● Permafrost works like a giant freezer. In Siberia it has preserved the bodies of mammoths for thousands of years. Many of these prehistoric elephants have been found in the frozen soil.

● In 1985 scientists dug up tree stumps from the permafrost on Axel Heiberg Island in the Canadian Arctic. The scientists thought the stumps were about 45 million years old. These ancient stumps could still be cut up and burned!

The coldest, wettest, and driest areas of tundra have poor soil. Because few plants can take root there, very few leaves fall to the ground, where they can rot and enrich the soil. The soil remains thin or gravelly in these areas. However, nearer the warmer southern edge of the Arctic tundra, the climate is less harsh. More plants grow and more animals live there. Rotting plants and animal droppings help to make the soil richer and deeper.

Geography Detective

What happens to waterlogged soil when it freezes? You can find out by filling a plastic container with water and soil. Put the container in the freezer and see what happens. What can happen at home if water freezes in a pipe?

This house in the Canadian tundra is sinking into the ground. Why do you think this is happening?

Tundra Wetlands

Large areas of the Arctic tundra are wet and marshy. In summer shallow pools often form on the surface. Very little precipitation falls in tundra areas, so where does this water come from?

Most of the water appears when the frozen water in the surface soil thaws out. This water is called meltwater. Because the inactive layer of permafrost remains frozen, the meltwater in the active layer cannot drain into the ground below. By the end of summer, the wind and the sun have dried out many of these surface pools. Deeper pools are more permanent. They form shallow lakes, which freeze solid during the long winter.

Waterweeds, rushes, and **algae** grow in many of the pools, lakes, and marshes. Billions of tiny

▲ Meltwater and river water spill over the tundra. This is the Lena River in Siberia during the summer thaw.

▶ A spongy plant called sphagnum moss (right) grows in tundra pools. The moss forms layers of matted vegetation, which can fill the pool and create a **muskeg**. The vegetation decays over time, forming a peat bog. Bogs are found in both the Antarctic and the Arctic tundra regions.

▶ The marshy, muddy lands near the seacoasts of the Arctic tundra are called salt marshes. When the ocean is not frozen, seawater covers the salt marshes during **high tides**. Many salt-loving plants grow in the marshes, and birds and other wildlife live there. These eider ducks are standing near salt marshes in Greenland.

● A lot of water in the world's tundra zone is locked up in huge masses of ice called **glaciers**.

● Sphagnum moss is so spongy that it can soak up ten times its own weight in water.

insects, such as mosquitoes and blackflies, breed in these wetlands.

Water in the tundra also comes from rivers that cross the landscape on their way to the Arctic Ocean. In winter the rivers freeze. But in summer, when the ice melts, the rivers often burst their banks and flood the land.

Geography Detective

Can you spot the red-throated diver in this picture? Why do you think many birds visit the pools on the tundra in summer? What might they feed on in the pools? Why would they not visit the tundra during the winter months?

Tundra Plants

Plants need sunlight and warmth to grow. The Arctic growing season is very short, though, lasting only two or three months. The plants grow quickly during the summer, when there may be 20 hours of sunlight each day. Tundra plants have to be tough to survive the harsh winters and the strong, cold winds. Most of these plants are very low-growing. They hug the frozen ground or find shelter in cracks.

Tundra plants include grasses, mosses, and many types of lichens. Lichens need little soil and grow on the surface of the ground or form crusty patches on rocks. In warmer or sheltered areas, small shrubs such as crowberry and bilberry thrive. Dwarf willows, rushes, sedges, and cottongrass grow near pools and bogs.

During the short summer, the tundra suddenly bursts into flower with colorful poppies, purple saxifrage, Arctic bluebells, and campions.

Very few trees can survive on the tundra. Sometimes you might see alders, willows, or birches. Spruces may grow in the warmer southern tundra.

▲ Mosses and lichens grow in the Arctic tundra. Lichens are made up of two kinds of plants—algae and **fungi**. Reindeer moss grows over poor soil, gravel, and rocks. Caribou depend on this lichen for much of their food.

► Bearberries and other shrubs bring bright patches of color to Denali National Park in Alaska. Some people use the shrub's leaves as medicine. Both people and animals eat the plant's red berries.

- Yellow poppies and Arctic willows grow in the world's most northern lands.

- About 250,000 species (kinds) of flowering plants grow on earth. Most of them thrive in warm, tropical regions. Only about 500 species of wildflowers can survive on Greenland's tundra.

In the past, the peoples who lived in the Arctic tundra region used plants in many ways to survive. They ate berries and made medicines from herbs and leaves. They stacked sod (blocks of earth and grass) to build shelters. In some places, mosses were used for diapers!

▼ Tundra plants are survivors. They push through the melting snow and bring color to the landscape in summer.

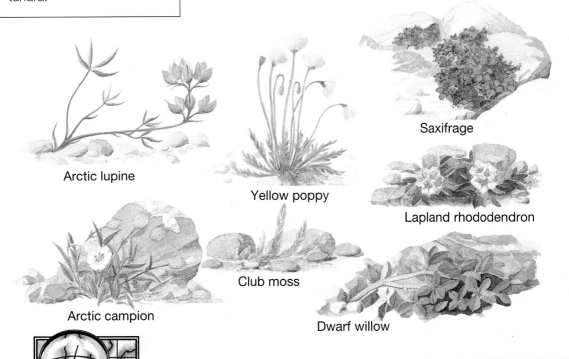

Arctic lupine

Yellow poppy

Saxifrage

Lapland rhododendron

Club moss

Arctic campion

Dwarf willow

Geography Detective

Why do you think this tree cannot put down deep roots on the tundra? Why is it so stunted? What does frost do to buds and new shoots? How does the rock protect the tree?

Tundra Wildlife

A willow grouse blends in with the green and brown colors of the summer tundra. This camouflage, or disguise, hides prey from the animals that hunt them. It also hides hunters from their prey.

Many different kinds of wildlife make their homes on the tundra. Some birds live in the Arctic tundra all year. Snow buntings feed on seeds, and rock ptarmigan eat shoots and berries. Ravens eat carrion (the meat of dead animals) and birds' eggs. Snowy owls and gyrfalcons hunt small animals. Many small, plant-eating mammals, such as lemmings, hares, voles, weasels, and stoats, live on the tundra. Arctic foxes and pale-coated gray wolves hunt these smaller animals.

An Arctic fox runs across the tundra in Greenland. Like many Arctic animals, some kinds of Arctic fox have coats that turn white in winter. This makes the animals invisible against the snow and ice.

► Musk oxen eat tundra grasses. The animals' thick, heavy coats protect them from the winter winds.

● The real rulers of the tundra are tiny insects. One square yard of turf may be home to up to 1,000 jumping insects called springtails.

● Animals in alpine tundra regions include small, burrowing mammals, such as alpine marmots, which live in Europe, and chinchillas, which live in the Andes Mountains of South America.

Arctic waters are rich in fish and whales. Polar bears hunt seals, which breed along the coastlines of the Arctic tundra. Large, grazing mammals also roam the region. They include huge herds of caribou and powerful musk oxen.

How do tundra animals survive the winter? Hoary marmots hibernate in burrows through the long winter. Their bodies slow down and they sleep most of the time. Lemmings do not hibernate. They tunnel under the snow to keep warm. Snowy owls have downy feathers to keep them warm, while musk oxen have long, shaggy coats.

Geography Detective

Most owls nest in trees. Why do you think the snowy owl in this picture is nesting on the ground? Why would the owl need to see as much of the surrounding tundra as possible? Why are its feathers white and fluffy? Most owls hunt only at night. Why do• you think snowy owls can hunt during the day?

Reproduction and Migration

The animals that live on the tundra move around in search of food, water, and a safe place to have their young. They move mostly in summer. Many creatures also **migrate** onto the thawing tundra to feed, hunt, and breed. These visitors include wading birds, insect-eating birds, swans and ducks, brown bears, lynx, and coyotes. Whales migrate northward into Arctic waters as soon as the winter ice breaks up.

In years when there is plenty of food, animals such as lemmings and Arctic voles breed rapidly. One female may have as many as five sets of young in one summer, with five or six babies at a time. After two or three good summers, the tundra may swarm with lemmings. They pour across the ground in search of food and even swim across rivers and lakes. If the water is rough, thousands of lemmings may drown. When a hard winter comes, the number of lemmings falls.

▲ Birds of prey such as the rough-legged buzzard hunt collared lemmings (above). If the number of lemmings falls, the number of buzzards will also fall.

Sometimes a harsh winter may follow a short, cold summer, leaving very little food on the tundra. Many small animals die of hunger.

● The Arctic tern is a seabird that fishes off the coasts of the tundra region. Between breeding seasons, terns fly to Antarctica, a journey of more than 23,000 miles. This is the longest migration that scientists know about.

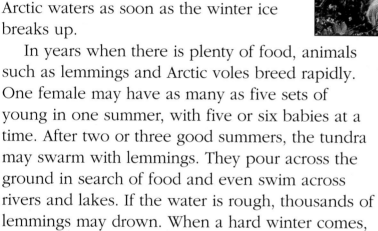

◄ Snow geese from the tundra migrate to California for the winter. In spring the geese fly north again to breed.

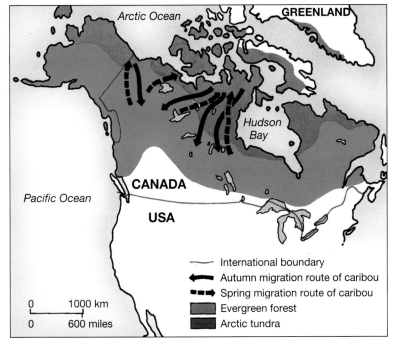

◀ Each spring barren-ground caribou migrate by the thousands onto the Arctic tundra from forests to the south. The animals make a round trip of more than 6,000 miles each year.

◀ This map shows the migration pattern of barren-ground caribou in Canada.

Map labels: Arctic Ocean, GREENLAND, Hudson Bay, CANADA, USA, Pacific Ocean

Legend:
— International boundary
← Autumn migration route of caribou
◄■■► Spring migration route of caribou
▦ Evergreen forest
▓ Arctic tundra

0   1000 km
0   600 miles

Geography Detective

Migrating animals live in many parts of the world. Birds in your neighborhood may have come from far away. The geese and ducks you see in local parks or on lakes, for example, may breed in the far north. Use a bird book to find the names of birds that live in your area. Which birds do you see only in the summer? Where do they go in the winter? Which birds visit only in winter? Where have they come from?

Case Study

Each summer more than one million barren-ground caribou migrate onto the Canadian tundra. During the winter, the animals shelter in the forests to the south. In spring they gather in huge herds and start their migration to the tundra. Caribou calves are born on the way. Hungry wolves, who feed on caribou, follow the herds. The broad hooves of the caribou help to support them on snow and wet ground. They can scrape away melting snow from reindeer moss, which they eat. In winter the caribou make the long journey back to the forests.

19

Living on the Tundra

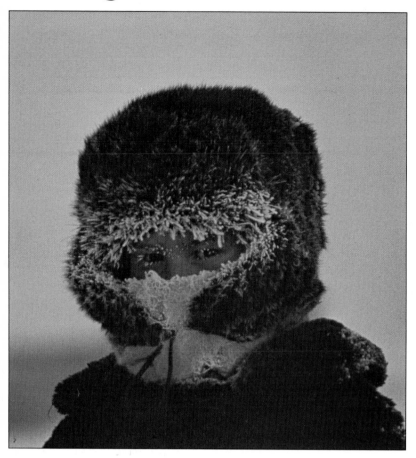

◀ In the Arctic tundra, people must wear warm clothing outside to survive the cold winters. If they don't, they face serious risks. **Frostbite**, for example, freezes and damages flesh. **Hypothermia**, which can cause death, occurs when the body's temperature drops too low.

People have made their homes on the tundra for thousands of years. The first tundra peoples lived in small, scattered groups. They were herders, hunters, and fishers, who relied on plants and animals for food and clothing. People made their homes from natural materials such as animal skins, stones, sod, and even blocks of snow. Their way of life provided everything they needed.

Gradually other people came to the tundra. Explorers came to find routes to other lands. Traders came to buy furs. Prospectors discovered coal, gold, and other minerals. The newcomers opened mines and built towns. But they also brought problems, since they did not always respect the tundra peoples' way of life.

● In the 1800s, European and American whalers went to the Canadian Arctic to hunt whales. At that time, baleen (whalebone) was used in women's corsets (undergarments). Whale blubber was boiled to make fuel for lamps. But like other newcomers, whalers brought diseases, which killed many native peoples of the tundra.

These skidoos are being checked over at Cambridge Bay in the Canadian Arctic. Skidoos are common throughout the Arctic. People once relied on dogs to haul sleds across the tundra. Today dogs are rarely used.

Nowadays roads, airlines, and communication systems link the peoples of the tundra with one another and with lands to the south. People on the tundra live in settled communities and make a living at wage-earning jobs. Some native people still spend part of the year hunting and fishing. For most native peoples, though, their way of life is very different from the way their ancestors lived.

Geography Detective

People who live in the Canadian Arctic travel by airplane more often than people who live in southern Canada. Why do you think this is? Why is it more difficult to travel by land or sea in the north?

Young people buy ice cream from a store in Savissavik, Greenland. Modern settlements and communications have changed life in the Arctic tundra. Television and radio stations broadcast programs in local, native languages. People also use the Internet, which allows computer users to find information and to exchange messages with people all over the world.

Peoples of the Tundra

Many different native groups make their homes on the Arctic tundra. They speak different languages and follow different ways of life. But they all share a love of the land and pride in their cultures.

The Sami, or Lapps, live in Lapland in northern Scandinavia. In the past, they herded reindeer for food and clothing material. Today few Sami families follow that way of life. Much of their land has been taken over by mining and power companies. Many Sami now have jobs in the fishing or forestry industries.

The tundra in Russia is home to 28 different groups. They include the Dolgan, Komi, Nentsi, Mansi, Khanti, Yakuts, Yukhaghir, and Chukchi. These peoples once lived by herding reindeer, trading, and hunting. However, over the past 100 years, large areas of their land have been seized for mining and other industries.

About 16,000 years ago, peoples from Siberia settled in the North American Arctic. Indian peoples called these northerners *askimek* or

▲ This Chukchi family lives in eastern Siberia. In the past, the Russian government banned the languages of the Arctic peoples of this region. Today the native people do have more rights. However, they still face great hardship and are still very poor.

● Greenland is the least crowded land in the world. Only 57,000 people live in an area of more than 700,000 square miles. That is about one person for every 15 square miles.

◀ A Sami herder in Swedish Lapland counts reindeer. Lapland includes territory in Norway, Sweden, Finland, and Russia. Since 1993 the Sami in Sweden have had their own *Sameting*, or government body.

eskimantis, which means "eaters of raw meat." European explorers later called them Eskimos. But these native Arctic peoples call themselves Inuit, which means "the people." This is the term most widely used today.

▼ In 1992 the Inuit of Arctic Canada and the Canadian government agreed that the Inuit would have their own territory, called Nunavut (see map), starting in 1999. The agreement gives the Inuit ownership of part of the land in Nunavut and joint control over the rest. The Inuit have the right to hunt, fish, and trap throughout the territory. They also control the mining of copper, gold, silver, and other minerals in the area.

▲ This Inuit child lives in the Thule district of Greenland, or Kalaallit Nunaat as it is known in the local language. An island region of Denmark, Greenland has governed itself since 1981.

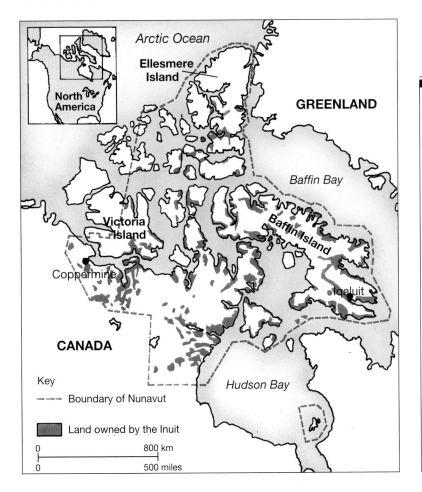

Key

- - - Boundary of Nunavut

▓ Land owned by the Inuit

0 ——— 800 km
0 ——— 500 miles

Geography Detective

These words for the months of the year are from the Inuit language Inuktitut. The words tell us a lot about life in the far north. January is called *Sekiliniak,* which means "the sun appears." May is *Agpaliarssuit tikitarfiat,* or "the birds return." September is *Talsit sikoutat,* or "the lakes freeze." Can you invent some names for months that describe where *you* live? Examples might be "the trees are bare," "the rain falls in buckets," or "the tourists go home."

Tundra Industries

The wealth of the Arctic lies underground, where rich supplies of oil, coal, and natural gas are found. Big companies also mine gold, diamonds, zinc, lead, and copper. When the Inuit and other native peoples claim their rights to the land, they hope they will benefit from the jobs and wealth that come to their region.

But mining in the Arctic is difficult and very expensive. Seaports freeze up for most of the year, so workers and machinery must be flown in to the area's mines. Oil and gas must be piped out over huge distances. And the environment must be protected. For example, underground oil production pipes and aboveground pipelines get very hot. They must be insulated, or protected, so the heat does not escape and melt the permafrost.

● The Trans-Alaska oil pipeline runs 800 miles across the Alaskan tundra from Prudhoe Bay to the port of Valdez in southern Alaska.

● The Alaska pipeline crosses three mountain chains, as well as 600 rivers and streams. In some places, it is raised high above the ground so that migrating caribou can pass underneath.

◀ This woman is working in a fish factory at Tromso, Norway. Fishing is an important industry in the Arctic. The catch provides fish for local people to eat and to sell to other countries.

● Norwegian and Russian companies mine coal on the Arctic island of Spitsbergen. Spitsbergen is one of a group of islands called Svalbard, which Norway governs. The world's most northern settlement—Ny Ålesund—lies on the coast of Spitsbergen above the latitude of 78° North.

Tourism is a new and growing industry in the Arctic tundra. People visit the area for kayaking, hiking, and watching birds and whales. The Inuit and other native peoples make money from tourists by selling artwork and crafts they make themselves. These goods are also sold in shops around the world.

▼ Prudhoe Bay is an oil-production base on the north coast of Alaska. Oil worth billions of dollars is piped south from the bay and is then shipped to ports in British Columbia, Washington, and California. While icy winds blow outside, the operation centers at Prudhoe Bay are warm and cosy. Workers inside can play sports. They can even enjoy indoor parks full of trees and plants that would not survive outside.

Geography Detective

Imagine you have to build an oil pipeline across the Arctic tundra. Why would it be hard to build or repair the pipe? What kinds of problems with the soil might you expect? Why might you want to put some sections of the pipe high above the ground?

Environment at Risk

◀ Seal pups have been slaughtered by the hundreds of thousands because some people say they threaten fish, which are important to the economy of the Arctic tundra. New laws are now helping to control the killing of many wild animals.

Different forms of pollution threaten the tundra environment. Building roads and mines disturbs tundra soils. Waste from metal and chemical industries pollutes these soils. Winds carry **acid snow** from factories that lie far to the south. This snow poisons the tundra land and streams and threatens wildlife. And dumping **nuclear waste** threatens to make Siberian waters **radioactive**.

Scientists believe the world's climate is slowly becoming warmer from exhaust fumes that trap heat in the earth's atmosphere. This **global warming** might melt Arctic glaciers, which would raise sea levels and change the tundra climate.

Case Study

The tundra of western Siberia, which borders the Kara Sea, is a beautiful wilderness. The region is rich in plants

▼ A ski lift takes skiers in Alaska to the top of the slopes. Nature reserves and national parks attract many tourists to the Arctic tundra. The reserves also help to protect the tundra and its wildlife.

and wildlife. However, pollution from industries is threatening this area. Waste and rusting oil drums litter the settlements. Chemicals poison the wildlife, and metal wastes pollute the rivers. The wind brings deadly pollution from the factory smokestacks of Norilsk, Russia, which lies to the south of the tundra. Norilsk is the world's biggest producer of nickel, cobalt, and copper.

In 1993 the Great Arctic Reserve was created to protect the west Siberian tundra. The reserve is about the size of Switzerland. It is home to wildlife such as polar bears, walrus, and beluga whales.

● Ice-breaker ships keep the Arctic seas between Murmansk, Russia, and the Bering Strait to the east open for about four months each year. As more oil tankers travel these waters, the risk of spillages increases.

◄ Workers clean up oil after the oil tanker *Exxon Valdez* spilled 11 million gallons of thick, black oil into the sea off the southern coast of Alaska in 1989. Scientists estimate that more than 300,000 seabirds alone died as a result of this spill. Many other types of animals and plants also died.

Geography Detective

Industries bring money and jobs to areas where people need work. But these industries can also bring problems. They may damage the environment, for example. What if oil was found in a national wildlife refuge? Do you think the government should allow companies to drill for oil there? Why or why not?

Mapwork

1. Look at the map on the opposite page and find the letters A, B, C, D, and E. Now look at the pictures below, which are labeled 1, 2, 3, 4, and 5. Can you match the pictures to the letters?

2. Use the map to answer the following questions:
   a) Where do you think oil is produced?
   b) From where do you think oil is transported out of the region?
   c) What would be the quickest way to travel from Tugtossuak to Safe Haven?
   d) How far is it by road from Tugtossuak to Safe Haven?

3. a) Where would wildlife be strictly protected?
   b) What kinds of wildlife might migrate to Copper Lake in the summer?
   c) Where might the caribou go in winter?

1

2

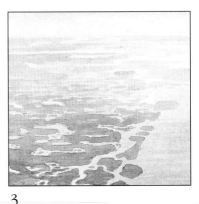

3

4

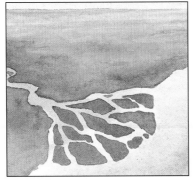

5

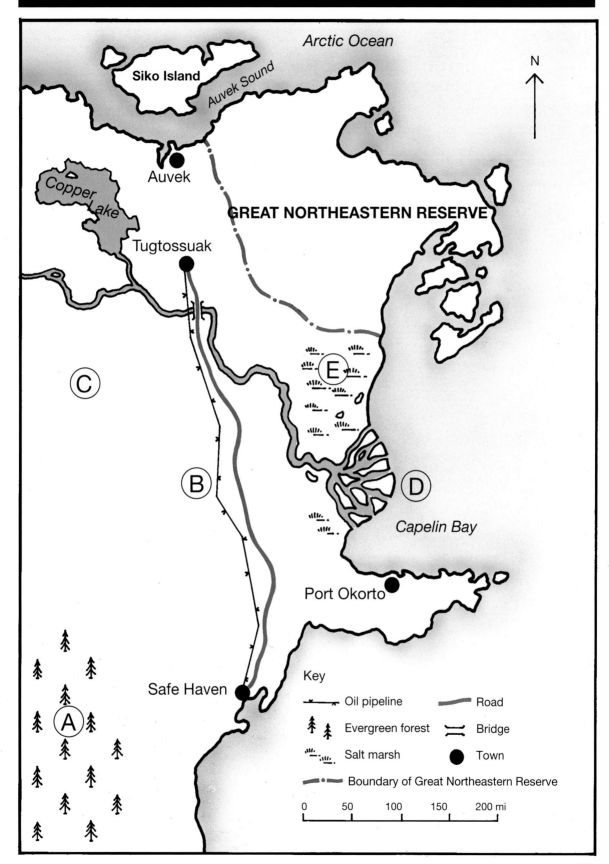

Arctic Ocean

Siko Island

Auvek Sound

Auvek

Copper Lake

Tugtossuak

GREAT NORTHEASTERN RESERVE

N

C

E

B

D

Capelin Bay

Port Okorto

Safe Haven

A

Key

Oil pipeline   Road

Evergreen forest   Bridge

Salt marsh   Town

Boundary of Great Northeastern Reserve

0   50   100   150   200 mi

Glossary

acid snow: Snow that contains chemical pollutants from the air.

active layer: The surface layer of tundra soil that thaws in summer.

algae: Simple forms of plant life that grow in water.

drought: A long period without rain or snow.

equator: The line that circles maps and globes at 0° of latitude.

frostbite: Damage caused to skin by extreme cold.

fungi: Plants such as molds, mildews, or mushrooms.

glacier: A huge mass of ice that moves slowly over the land. Glaciers may be several miles thick.

global warming: An increase in the world's average temperature. Many scientists believe this is caused by the exhaust fumes from burning fossil fuels such as coal and oil. The gas in these fumes traps heat in the atmosphere.

high tide: The highest point reached by the surface of the sea. This occurs twice daily.

hypothermia: A condition in which the body temperature falls below the usual level.

inactive layer: The lower layer of tundra soil, which never thaws.

latitude: Lines that mapmakers draw on maps and globes to divide up the surface of the earth. Lines of latitude circle the earth. They measure, in degrees, the distance north or south from the equator, which circles the globe at 0° of latitude.

longitude: Lines on maps and globes that run from the North Pole to the South Pole. Lines of longitude are measured in degrees and lie either to the east or west of 0° longitude, which runs through London, England.

migrate: To travel from one region to another for feeding or breeding.

muskeg: A tundra wetland containing layers of sphagnum moss.

nuclear waste: Waste materials that give off dangerous rays of energy called radiation.

ocean current: A movement of the surface water of an ocean caused mainly by winds.

patterned ground: An area of tundra where repeated freezing and thawing have created cracks, ridges, and hollows.

permafrost: Permanently frozen soil.

pingo: A hump of soil that is pushed up when an underground pool of water freezes.

polygon: A many-sided depression or crater that is formed on the tundra by repeated freezing and thawing of water in the soil.

precipitation: Water that falls to the ground as rain, snow, hail, or sleet.

radioactive: Giving off dangerous rays of energy called radiation.

snow line: The height on a mountain slope above which there is always snow and ice.

solifluction: The slow creeping of waterlogged soil down a slope.

taiga: The belt of forestland lying to the south of the Arctic tundra. The trees are mostly coniferous (cone-bearing) evergreens, such as spruces and firs.

tree line: The point on a mountain slope or in the lowlands of the far north above which conditions are too harsh for trees to grow.

wetland: An area containing much wet soil. Wetlands include marshes, swamps, bogs, and the shorelines of rivers and lakes.

METRIC CONVERSION CHART		
WHEN YOU KNOW	**MULTIPLY BY**	**TO FIND**
inches	25.4	millimeters
inches	2.54	centimeters
feet	0.3048	meters
miles	1.609	kilometers
square miles	2.59	square kilometers
acres	0.4047	hectares
gallons	3.78	liters
degrees Fahrenheit	.56 (after subtracting 32)	degrees Celsius

Index